DESTRUCTION AND RENEWAL

THE SYNAGOGUES OF THE JEWISH QUARTER

DESTRUCTION AND RENEWAL

THE SYNAGOGUES OF THE JEWISH QUARTER

by

SHIMON BEN-ELIEZER

Second revised edition

RUBIN MASS, JERUSALEM, 1975

Thanks are due to the friends of the late Dr. Shimon Ben-Eliezer in Israel and the United States who made possible the publication of the manuscript; and to the American-Israeli Paper Mills Ltd. Hadera, for its contribution.

Research and Editorial: Avraham Greenberg

Photographs: Werner Braun and The Jewish Agency Photo Service

Printed in Israel by Alpha Press, Jerusalem, 1975

CONTENTS

FOREWORD

This collection of sketches dealing with the
history of the most celebrated among the synagogues of
the Old City is a labour of love by a citizen of Jerusalem
who was stirred by the Six Day War into exploring and
documenting the antecedents of what was then a scene of
utter desolation and ruin. Sadly, the author did not live to
see the restoration to their former glory of at least some
of the buildings and sites he describes with such affection
and literary skill. Nor was he able to complete an intro-
ductory chapter he had planned to write. But from the
notes he left with the manuscript, it is apparent that he had
in mind to preface the sketches with a discussion of the
concept of "Holy Places" as he perceived it.

It was Ben-Eliezer's view that in a pure monotheism
there is no scope for such a notion, and in the notes he
makes the point that the term "hallowed places" would
be far more appropriate than "holy places." In the Jewish
tradition in particular, so ran his reasoning, the acceptance
of prayer is not conditioned by the place where it is offered.
Yet it is also true that the intensity of prayer may be

heightened by the associations of a place, and that these associations may bring about a religious experience not attainable elsewhere.

But even without the benefit of the intended introduction, the collection itself offers a wealth of information to the visitor — be he Jew or non-Jew — to the Old City and its Jewish Quarter. And in its overall impact, the booklet reflects the powerful attachment of the Jewish people to their Holy City, an attachment which manifested itself not merely in their daily prayers throughout the long exile, but also in the desire of many of them to live in Jerusalem or at least to visit it as pilgrims. The synagogues of the Jewish Quarter bore eloquent and concrete witness to that attachment until they were so wantonly razed to the ground.

But the author also makes it clear that, from the time of the Shomrei Hahomot — the stubborn Guardians of the Walls, there was a hiatus in Jewish settlement until the Ramban (Moses Nachmanides), the great commentator, philosopher and mystic came to Jerusalem from Spain in 1267 to find only two Jews there. He was followed by the great Mishna commentator Ovadia of Bartenura who arrived in 1488, and a bare 15 years after the expulsion from Spain there was already a sizable Sephardi community sustaining four synagogues, all linked with one another.

Interestingly enough, all of these synagogues were below street level, ostensibly "to gain loftiness by excavating the soil," but mainly because the Moslems objected to any synagogue which might overshadow a mosque. In one of the four, named after Yochanan Ben Zakkai, the sage who left the city clandestinely at the time of the Roman siege and helped perpetuate Judaism in his famous Academy of Yavneh, forty Sephardi chief rabbis were ordained in subsequent generations. For the original Sephardi settlers — survivors of the Inquisition of Spain — were later reinforced by North African Jews under the leadership of the Kabbalist Chaim Ibn Atar in 1736 and by Yemenites, led by Shalom Sharabi, in 1757.

The Ashkenazim, it is pointed out, were relative late-comers. In 1812 an epidemic broke out in the city of Safad which had attracted to it the disciples of the Gaon of Vilna, known as the Perushim, and many of them fled to Jerusalem to form the nucleus of the Ashkenazi com-munity there. The author vividly describes the formation of their Tiferet Yisrael synagogue which, though its con-struction was authorized by a *firman* from the Turkish au-thorities as early as 1858, was dedicated only in 1876. Then as now, it took time to raise the necessary funds. But few present-day endeavours of this kind can claim as distinguished a contributor as the Emperor Franz Joseph I of Austria, who made a donation to the building fund of Tiferet Yis-rael.

The main Ashkenazi synagogue, the Hurva (Ruin) of Rabbi Yehuda he-Chassid, was the scene of a historic occa-sion when the first British High Commissioner for Pales-tine, Sir Herbert Samuel, walked there from his official residence a few days after his investiture and recited the Haftarah of the "Sabbath of Comfort." Overcome by the significance of the moment, the Jew Samuel wept as he read the benediction, "Suffer not a stranger to sit upon his throne, nor let others any longer inherit his glory."

In discussing the Karaite synagogue, the author observes that the Karaites were the Orthodox of their time when they emerged in the 8th century, and that it was the Rabbanites who were then the reformers. But in the course of time the latter became the Orthodox, ostracizing the Karaites who maintained a community in Jerusalem since the 11th century. Its membership had shrunk to insignificance when it was reinforced by Karaite immigration from Egypt in 1957.

Now that the Jewish Quarter is being rebuilt, and the four Sephardi synagogues at least have been restored, it is doubly valuable to have in this booklet a record, both pictorial and textual, of the state of devastation in which the Quarter was found in 1967. For even if all the 65 synagogues, the Yeshivot, hospitals and other charitable institutions were resurrected, and the Jewish Quarter once again inhabited by Jews, it would still be fitting that in our joy and comfort we remember the destruction, as we are bid by our tradition.

Rabbi Moses Cyrus Weiler

RIGHT IN THE HEART OF WHAT USED TO BE THE Jewish Quarter rises a slender minaret. Intended as a challenge to the stubborn infidels, it serves as a landmark of the most ancient synagogue within the walls.

The origins of this place of worship are lost in antiquity. There is reason to believe, however, that the Gaonim may have prayed and taught on this very spot as early as the Tenth Century. Romanesque vaults resting on Roman and Byzantine capitals and the complete absence of Gothic or late Moslem features suggest that the building must date back to pre-Crusader times.

For the past 700 years it has been known as the Ramban Synagogue. There is documentary proof of its reconstruction by the great pilgrim from Spain who revived Jewish settlement in the Holy Land after the conquest of Jerusalem by the Tartars and the expulsion of the Crusaders. As the Rabbi wrote to his son Nachman, he set foot in the Holy City on the 9th of Elul, 5027, (September 1, 1267) and this is what he found:

"What shall I tell you about the land but that its desertion is great and its desolation complete. In brief, the more sacred a place, the worse its prostration: Judea more so than Galilee and Jerusalem most of all. Yet for all its destruction the city is very good and has close to two thousand inhabitants, among them three hundred Christians saved from the Sultan's sword. But there are no Jews in it, for they have fled since the coming of the Tartars or fallen to their sword, save for two brothers, dyers by their calling, in whose rooms a *minyan* gathers on the Sabbaths. And now... we have found a dilapidated house, built on marble pillars and with a beautiful dome, and taken it as a synagogue, for the city is derelict and whosoever wants to take possession of its ruins may do so. We have vowed to repair the house and have already started work and sent to Nablus to bring back Torah scrolls which were formerly in Jerusalem..."

Two centuries later a poignant change takes place. As another pious traveller, the renowned Mishna commentator Rabbi Ovadia of Bartenura, recounts in 1488, a minaret now dominates the courtyard of the ancient synagogue. "The house next to it formerly belonged to a Jew, and because of a quarrel and dispute with his fellows this man became a Moslem. And when his mother saw that her son had abandoned his faith on account of all the anguish caused to him by the Jews, she rose up and vowed her house in the synagogue courtyard as a place of abomination for the Ismaelites and built a mosque on it to take her revenge on the Jews. This is what brought about all the evil that followed. The synagogue lay waste until by the grace of God the King commanded, against the will of his princes and servants and of all the people in his land, to build the house again and rear it even more than before." We know in

RAMBAN SYNAGOGUE
"a delapidated house, built on marble pillars"

CHURVA SYNAGOGUE
"serves-as a landmark of the most ancient synagogue"

"all of a sudden an aged stranger walked in" —
Entrance to the Prophet Elijah Synagogue

Istanbul Synagogue
Part of a plaque (1836)

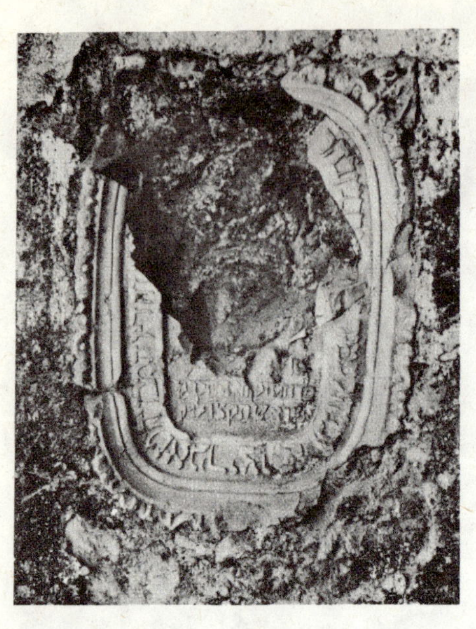

Used for temporary housing (1948–1967)

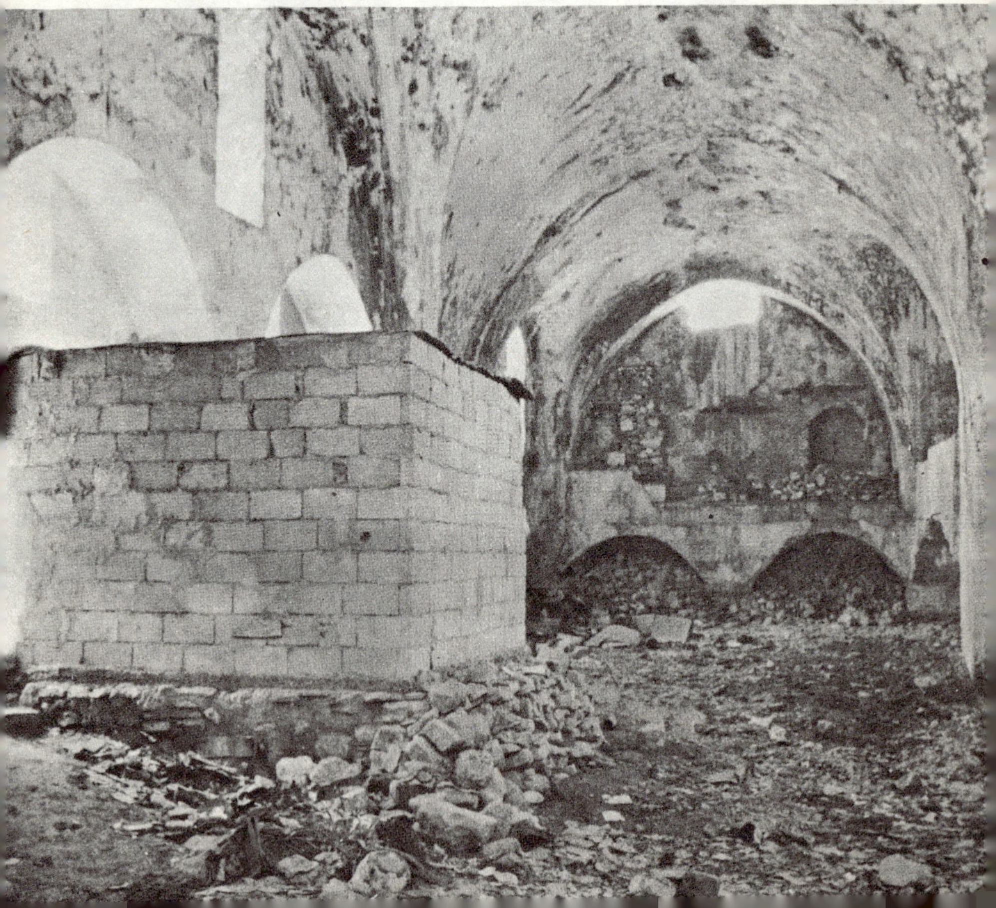

fact from another source that in this context the Kadi of Jerusalem and other Moslem notables were carried in chains to the Court of Cairo.

A description of the rebuilt synagogue in 1523, by Rabbi Moshe Bassula, refers to it as the only Jewish place of worship in Jerusalem, facing the Temple Mount, with a row of four pillars and more than 60 Torah scrolls, but lacking windows and only lit by candles.

In the course of time repeated attempts were made to dispute the Jewish ownership of the place. According to one source, "there came a Mufti, a hater of the faith, and ordered the synagogue to be closed down, for it once had been sanctified as a mosque, and the Jews could not restore it and the place served for all manners of profanity. And when the Elders heard of this, they sent to the Judge asking him not to lay hands on the sanctity of the synagogue which Israel had bought for good money, and showed him the purchase deed duly signed. But he would not let off until they paid him one thousand Grush and obtained a ruling of his court saying that no man shall hinder them from praying there at any time they please."

Which did not, however, prevent further similar extortions, as in 1586 when 200 ducats had to be paid to the Kadi for reconfirmation of the Jewish rights. Notwithstanding this *firman* the Arabs again took possession of the place and converted it into a flour mill. Even under the British Mandate sheep were kept on the premises, with the minaret serving as a police station.

The liberation of the Old City in 1967 at last enabled the Jews to recover their rightful property and to reopen the synagogue in the presence of the President of Israel precisely seven hundred years after its dedication by the Ramban.

THE COMPLEX OF FOUR
SEPHARDI SYNAGOGUES:
YOHANAN BEN ZAKKAI; PROPHET ELIJAH;
THE MIDDLE SYNAGOGUE;
KEHAL ISTANBUL

IN 1517 SELIM I CONQUERED JERUSALEM FROM THE
Mamelukes and the city passed from Egyptian to Ottoman
rule, which was to last exactly four hundred years. Following in the footsteps of Saladin, who had ousted the Crusaders in 1187, the new masters took a favourable view of
Jewish settlement. They hoped, no doubt, that Jewish
energy and enterprise might contribute to a revival of the
desolate land. Circumstances were auspicious, for in the
wake of their expulsion from Spain by Ferdinand the
Catholic twenty-five years earlier, Jews were again on the
move, casting about for a haven of refuge, and many had
turned to Constantinople.

It thus came about that a sizable Sephardi community
developed in Jerusalem. Their first concern, as always in
Jewish history, was to set up a house of prayer, and before
long four synagogues, all linked with one another, arose
in what was to become the Jewish Quarter. "Arose" is
perhaps not the proper word to use, for they were in fact
built deep into the ground. Moslem law did not permit to
rear them above the level of ordinary houses. Therefore,

to observe the Talmudic injunction that a synagogue must excel all other structures in height, the builders decided to gain the required loftiness by excavating the soil. The result obtained was somewhat reminiscent of catacombs. It gave rise to popular belief that the intention was to recall the Psalmist's verse, "Out of the depths have I cried unto thee, O Lord."

For centuries the complex used to be known as the Yohanan Ben Zakkai synagogue, although strictly speaking the name applied to only one of the four prayer houses. But such looseness of nomenclature mattered little. The historical memories associated with this name outweighed all other considerations. Rabban Yohanan Ben Zakkai was the last sage to teach in Jerusalem before the destruction of the Second Temple. According to tradition, he had himself carried out of the besieged city in a coffin and later obtained permission from the victorious Romans to spare the yeshiva of Yavne — thereby ensuring the survival of Jewish learning and ultimately of the Jewish nation. Until the fall of Jerusalem the rabbi headed the "Big House," as his academy was called, a building described in the Talmud as one hundred ells high and casting its shadow right on to the Temple Mount. Although there is no archaeological evidence the belief long persisted that it was on this site that the four synagogues were erected.

The Yohanan Ben Zakkai wing proper, also referred to as the Kehal Talmud Torah, served as a venue for public functions. It was here that important business was transacted, visiting dignitaries were received and more than forty Sephardi chief rabbis elected and inducted into office.

Two precious relics added lustre to the place. In a pigeon-hole high up the southern wall there reposed an ancient oil jug and at its side a shofar. Both were reputed to have been saved from the burning Temple in anticipation of its resurrection. When in the fullness of time the Messiah came, his harbinger, the Prophet Elijah, would claim the oil to light the eternal flame and blow the shofar to herald the deliverance of Israel. Woe befall the nefarious hand daring to touch these objects.

Another miraculous tale tells of a blood libel related to this synagogue. Once a gentile infant was found slain before the Holy Ark, but Rabbi Kalonymus revived the child, thereby preventing the intended slaughter of the Jewish community. A rounded hollowed stone jutting out of the wall was believed to be a memorial to the shattered skull restored by the rabbi with the help of the Holy Name. The same significance was attributed to a stone tablet preserved in the Ark on which the four sacred letters of the Name were inscribed together with a seven-branched candelabrum. The tale no doubt reflects the ruthless oppression and systematic blackmail to which Jerusalem's Jews became subject in the 17th century, culminating in accusations of ritual murder seven years after the notorious blood libel of Damascus in 1840.

A second and somewhat older wing of the synagogue bore the name of the Prophet Elijah. It was built in 1586 after the enforced closing down of the Ramban prayer house. An inscription discovered in the course of repair works in 1880 suggests that its origins actually go back to the latter half of the 15th century; it may therefore have been erected on the foundations of an earlier building.

Various legendary explanations are offered for the naming of this synagogue, some obviously originating in the time when the congregation was at its lowest ebb. One Kol

Nidre night, it is told, only nine men could be found for prayer and there seemed no way of starting the service — until all of a sudden an aged stranger walked in to complete the *minyan* (the required quorum of ten). After the last Amen the stranger disappeared as miraculously as he had come, and all realized that they had been honored by the presence of the prophet.

Furthermore, in the north-western corner of the synagogue was a recess through which a few stairs led down to a cave, also called after Elijah. At its back stood, barely visible in the dim light of the eternal flame, an old armchair on which the wondrous figure is said to have once been seen. This chair served for the *brith mila* ritual among the Sephardi community. The father of the child would be seated on it, holding his son for circumcision, after intoning the verse "If I forget thee, O Jerusalem". — Throughout the ceremony a choir would chant joyous melodies, and at one stage the beadle would pass round branches of rosemary for the assembled to smell and pronounce the prescribed blessing on it.

Another remarkable seat, known as the Bridegroom's Chair, stood next to the Holy Ark. Covered with an elaborately carved canopy in Spanish renaissance style, it had been brought over from Spain by the refugees. Following a custom going back to that country, every bridegroom of the congregation was accorded the privilege of occupying it on his wedding day. On this occasion the chief rabbi and his court, together with the bridegroom's family, would assemble in the synagogue for *mincha* prayers to betake themselves hereafter in festive procession to the house of the bride.

Perhaps the most charming, and certainly a unique, piece

of equipment this prayer house boasted was a water sprinkling contrivance, described by a traveller in 1838. It was set in motion on the Feast of Tabernacles for *Simchat Beit Hasho'eva* — the Water Drawing ceremony — to recall the ancient rites of supplication for the blessing of rain.

The third wing, Kehal Istanbul, originally served the immigrants from Turkey and in particular from Constantinople (Istanbul). It later passed into the use of the Jews from Kurdistan. The most spacious of the four halls, it became a natural meeting place for the Sabbath afternoon crowds, including the womenfolk, who flocked there to hear the rabbi's sermon, in the Ladino vernacular, on the weekly portion of the law.

It also had the distinction of housing the *geniza*, a storeroom for unserviceable Torah scrolls, mutilated prayer books and other discarded religious texts pending their formal burial. At prescribed intervals a solemn funeral cortege would set out from here for the Mount of Olives or the slopes of Mount Zion.

In the winter of 1787 its roof caved in under a heavy weight of snow which had accumulated in an unprecedented storm of five successive days. Many years elapsed before permission was obtained to repair the damage, the worshippers suffering great hardship in the meantime.

The last of the four parts, called the Middle Synagogue, was a small-scale reproduction of the Yohanan Ben Zakkai wing, with exquisite Turkish stone ornaments over its gate. A secret tunnel was believed to lead from it to Mount Zion, outside the city walls.

The story goes that in days of yore there was an old Jewess who, peddling her wares among the gentile women on Mount Zion, took it into her head to set eyes on the royal tombs of the David dynasty. Her Arab friends protested that this was impossible and warned that she might risk her life in the attempt. They nevertheless suggested that she might gain entrance to the shrine on a Friday when all Moslems would be at service in the mosque. Suspecting no evil, the woman took the advice and was duly let into the cave by her reputed friends. But hardly had she crossed the threshold when the doors were bolted behind her: the design was to convert her to Islam on pain of death. Trapped and desperate, the woman threw herself into the dust, imploring King David for succor. And behold, the king appeared, speaking thus: "Fear not. Blessed art thou who hast been deemed worthy to stand on this ground. But beware lest thou let anyone know." With these words he conducted the awe-stricken woman safely out of the cave and led her through a deep shaft to this very synagogue where she continued to worship for many years after.

Occasional attempts at making proselytes indeed never ceased, despite the tolerance usually evinced by Moslem rulers. There always persisted a discrepancy between governmental enlightenment and popular fanaticism. Local leaders would often go out of their way to demonstrate their displeasure at rival religions. Right next to the Yohanan Ben Zakkai synagogue, for instance, they had a slaughterhouse installed, and near the Church of the Holy Sepulchre a tannery, so that an evil smell should ever plague the infidels.

Such pin-pricks notwithstanding, the Jews would lavish every care on their sanctuaries. Their women judged it a meritorious deed to sweep and polish even the approaches. No one who was privileged to see the Old City houses of prayer will ever forget their shining cleanness.

ONE OF THE FASCINATING ASPECTS OF OLD JERU-
salem is the intense interest its holy places have ever held
for the most varied historic figures, and the practical associations to which they have given rise. Men of striking
diversity have at one time or another come under the spell
of this unique city and found a common denominator in
contributing to its enhancement. Take, for instance, the
Churva, a compound of three Ashkenazi prayer houses,
with whose checkered fortunes kings and merchant princes,
saints and scholars, diplomats and politicians, artists and
artisans are inextricably bound up.

The first illustrious name associated with it is that of
Rabbi Judah he-Hasid of Poland. The saintly head of a
group of mystics, seekers of redemption through Cabbalistic studies and ascetic practices, he inspired his disciples
to follow him to the Promised Land. They set out on the
perilous journey in 1700 and, once in Jerusalem, took up
their abode in quarters prepared for them with funds sent
ahead. But the Rabbi did not live to see the fruits of his
labour. Barely three days after his arrival he passed away:

Ben Zakkai Synagogue

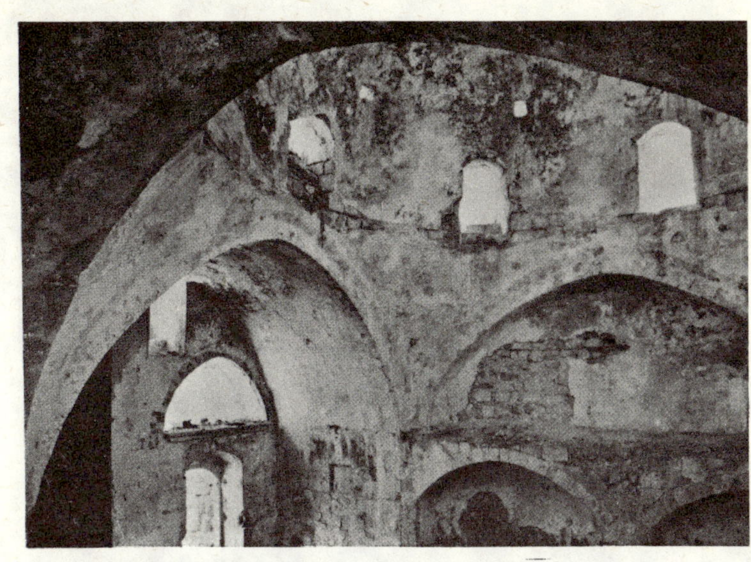

"More than 40 Chief Rabbis were elected—"

The Middle Synagogue — "a secret tunnel to Mount Zion"

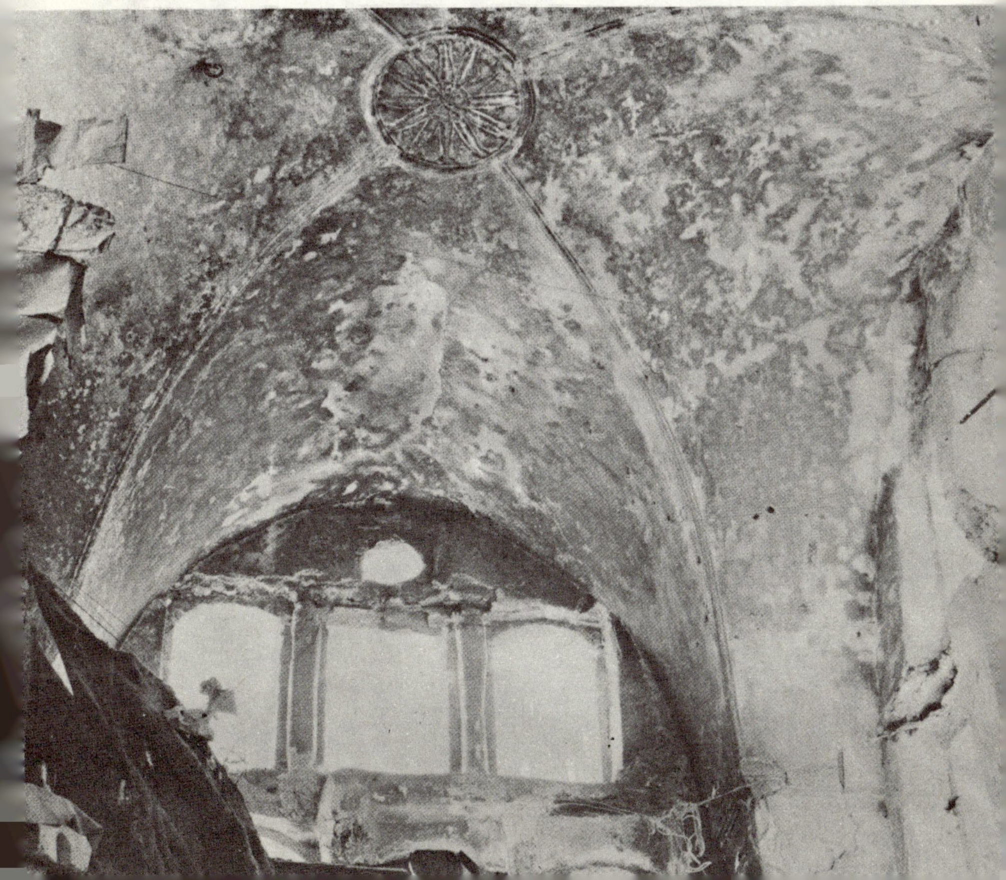

Jewish Quarter facing the Wailing Wall
(on far left: Porat Joseph Yeshiva)

TIFERET ISRAEL SYNAGOGUE (*before 1948*)

he had fallen ill after immersing himself in one of the mountain springs in honour of the approaching Sabbath.

The sudden loss of their leader brought disaster on the indigent community. Their sources of overseas support dried up, and they were no longer able to meet their commitments. Many started to drift away and some, in despair, forsook the faith of their fathers. The end came on a Sabbath day in 1720 when an irate crowd of creditors set upon the last remnants who had joined the earlier occupants of the compound, burning down the synagogue and driving all Ashkenazis out of the city. The catastrophe gave rise to the name of Churvat Rabbi Judah he-Hasid — "The Ruin" — by which the place has been known ever since.

It took another catastrophe to bring about the revival of Ashkenazi settlement in Jerusalem. In 1812 an epidemic spread through Galilee, and to escape its ravages some twenty disciples of the Gaon of Vilna made bold to seek refuge in Jerusalem. To conceal their identity, they put on Oriental garb, thereby gaining the right of residence which was not at that time denied to Sephardi Jews. To their relief they found the pressure for the repayment of the one hundred year old debt had meanwhile subsided; and indeed, final remission was granted by the Sublime Porte in 1820.

Paradoxically, those back to rebuild the Ashkenazi community at the Churva, the erstwhile center of Chassidism, were Perushim, the sworn enemies of that controversial sect. And it so turned out that henceforth the Churva compound became a symbol of strictly orthodox, rationalist Talmud Judaism.

In 1836 Abraham Shlomo Zalman Zoref, one of the prominent Perushim, went to Egypt to obtain a building permit from Mohamed Ali Pasha, founder of the new royal house, whose troops had crossed into Syria and taken possession of the holy cities a few years earlier. With energetic support from the Russian and Austrian consuls in Cairo, he succeeded in his delicate mission. A modest house of prayer, called Menachem Zion — "Comfort for Zion" — was promptly put up in the northern part of the compound. But the Moslems never forgave Rabbi Zoref for his daring: many years later they fell upon him on his way to early morning devotions and beat him to death.

One more catastrophe — the earthquake which devastated Safad in 1837 — brought another influx of Ashkenazim, and the need was felt for a further place of prayer. Ambitious plans sprang up for an impressive central synagogue, but meanwhile only a modest building could be erected. It was located on the southern end of the Churva, overlooking the adjacent Ramban synagogue which had passed into Arab hands in the 16th century. The name given to it, Sha'are Zion—"Gates of Zion" —is believed to have been chosen in rivalry with the near-by Kehal Zion — "Congregation of Zion" — where the earlier Ashkenazi Chassidim used to worship.

Meanwhile planning for the central synagogue proceeded apace. The site originally envisaged was near the Wailing Wall, but subsequently shifted to the Churva courtyard. In those very years the Sultan became subject to growing pressures by Russia as well as Great Britain and France in the wake of acrimonious and at times violent squabbles over the holy places. It was in these circumstances, and after the failure of numerous local and foreign notables over several years, that the British ambassador to the Porte, Lord Napier, intervened in 1854 and secured the issue of a *firman* (royal decree). One passage of the document, released over the signature of Sultan Abdul Mejid, merits quoting: "It is self-evident that justice and generosity alike enjoin that complete peace be assured to members of all faiths and religions dwelling in My sublime kingdom..."

Even so, the hard-won document was still withheld for reasons unknown to us. Another three years elapsed before it was handed to Sir Moses Montefiore as he was passing through Constantinople on the occasion of his fifth pilgrimage to the Holy Land, together with Lady Judith. It may be assumed that this eminent Jew of Italian origin, the first to attain social and political prominence in Britain, used his personal influence with the Sultan to have the *firman* delivered to him for formal submission to the Jerusalem authorities in 1857.

Excavation work for the foundations was promptly begun, notwithstanding repeated interferences by Moslem neighbours who sought to stop the building operations by force. An exciting discovery came to light while the plot was being cleared from the accumulated rubble of centuries — one of the two missing marble pillars which had borne the ancient Ramban synagogue. The relic was subsequently placed opposite the entrance to the new synagogue and became known in due course as "the column of care."

The honour of laying the foundation stone in 1858 went to Baron Alphonse de Rothschild, who besides his profound attachment to the Jewish people also had more mundane interests in the Middle East. As head of the Paris branch of Rothschild Brothers, he was later commissioned in conjunction with Ferdinand de Lesseps, builder of the Suez Canal, to effect a harmonization of French and British interests in this historic venture. His prominent participation in the ceremony was to herald the long and glorious association of his family with the rebuilding of the Jewish State.

From now on progress was sustained despite the costs involved. To raise the necessary funds — around one million Piasters — took considerable doing. Many and varied donors had to be approached in far-flung countries throughout the Jewish world. The arduous task naturally fell to the Jerusalem sponsors of the project, led by Joseph Yoel Rivlin and the above-mentioned Abraham Shlomo Zalman Zoref.

The largest single gift came from the "Rothschilds of the East." Yehezkel Reuben of Baghdad willed a sum of 100,000 Piasters, which was later augmented by his son, Rabbi Menasse, and his daughter, Lady Sassoon. Their combined donations, as testified by an inscription on the completed building, covered more than half of the outlay — surely a remarkable sidelight on the history of Sephardi-Ashkenazi relations.

Permission was also obtained from King Friedrich Wilhelm IV of Prussia to collect donations from his Jewish subjects. The purpose must have appealed to the poetic and religious sensitivity of this "Romantic on the Throne," who anticipated some of the traits of his better known scion Kaiser Wilhelm II. The man instrumental in arousing his interest was the great Hebrew scholar Michael Sachs, one of the early reform Rabbis who, incidentally sported a beard and skullcap and resigned from his Berlin congregation over their demand for having an organ installed. Both the king and the rabbi had their names recorded on a marble tablet, which did not, however, survive the synagogue's destruction by the Arabs.

In addition to the larger contributions a flow of small

CHURVA SYNAGOGUE
The Interior of the Dome (before 1948)

Churva Synagogue
The "Ruin" as seen in June 1967

"Fragments of a tablet were found" (dated 1837)

gifts, in cash and in kind, poured in from the lowly in the Diaspora as well as in Jerusalem. The slogan was, "Gain Eternal Life with one Stone." The most intriguing offering of all came from Pinchas Rosenberg, Imperial Court tailor of St. Petersburg. This is how he described with his own hand the details of his benefactions in the emissary's diary:

"... I give thanks to the Lord for his mercy with which he has moved my heart to donate to the holy building 100 Rubles and two big bronze candelabras, each with thirty-six branches to light the lamps thereof, at the cost of 80 Rubles. And I also donate a Hanuka candlestick 42 pounds in weight and three ells in height with eight branches, for which I spent 1,750 Rubles on silver work and 125 Rubles on transportation to Jerusalem through our dear emissary Rabbi Chaim Halevi, and this candlestick arrived miraculously on the 1st Tevet precisely in time to light the last eight Hanuka candles... whereupon I donated another 50 Rubles for candles and oil and a further 100 Rubles for cantors, beadles and Torah scribes and another 25 Rubles to have an iron door made under the Holy Ark for safe-keeping of the candlestick, and another 200 Rubles for the return of the above emissary and as a present to him. Altogether, with God's help, I spent on the above candle-stick 2,150 Rubles and another 28 Rubles on candles and oil for the two bronze candelabras. And now I offer my thanks to God who has enlightened my spirit to embellish the above house of worship by building an artistically wrought iron fence round the roof under the upper windows so that there be a veranda on which may stand all our brethren who go up in pilgrimage to behold our desolate Temple... and also a partition for the womenfolk on the Feast of Tabernacles and Simchat Torah..."

The Holy Ark, a work of elaborate craftsmanship, heavy with Baroque carvings set off against four Corinthian columns, and unique in having a reduced replica of it on top, was brought over complete from Cherson. It had there been the pride of Nikolaijewsky synagogue, the prayer house for ex-conscripts released after 25 years service in the Czarist army. The gates to the building were similarly brought from Russia, foreshadowing the transfer of entire synagogues, or parts of them, from Italy to Israel a century later.

After eight years of toil, presided over by the Jerusalem rabbi and artisan Mordechai Schnitzer, the house of worship could at last be dedicated in 1864. Officially named Beit Yaakov — "House of Jacob" — this most representative and imposing of all synagogues in the Old City never ceased, paradoxically, to be referred to as the Churva — "The Ruin."

In keeping with Jerusalem custom — Jewish, Christian and Moslem — the Churva compound always contained one or more houses for the accommodation of pilgrims. Rabbi Shmuel of Rogola, for instance, who donated 4,000 Piasters for the purpose in 1852, stipulated that in the hostel sponsored by him guests be entitled to an unlimited period of lodging as well as three days of free board. The residents of the city shared in the upkeep of the premises, each according to his capacity.

As time went on, the Churva became the centre of Jewish life in Jerusalem and the place of coronation for the Ashkenazi chief rabbis. It served as the natural depository for the flags of the Jewish Legion which took part in the conquest of Palestine by the British under General Allenby in 1917. It had its finest hour on the Sabbath of Comfort in 1920, when the first British High Commissioner, Sir Herbert Samuel, newly arrived at his seat of office, walked down from Government House to the venerable shrine to recite the weekly portion of prophetic readings, beginning on that memorable day with the words of Isaiah "Comfort ye, comfort ye my people, saith Your God; Bid Jerusalem take heart."

As fate would have it, all that remained of the Churva "Ruin" on June 7, 1967 was a heap of rubble. Under it, fragments of a tablet were found which had been affixed on one of the three houses of prayer laid waste with the compound. It read "This is the gate of the Lord which the righteous shall enter."

ASK ANY ONE FOR MODERN ISRAEL'S ORIGINAL GIFT to mankind, and you are likely to be told about the kibbutz. Plausible as it may seem, the answer yet fails to give credit to the numerous similar, if half-forgotten, attempts at communal living recorded in Jewish history.

Among the more recent ones is that associated with the Beit El congregation, which for nearly two centuries used to cluster around a few modest prayer rooms perched on the upper floor of a building owned jointly by Jews and Arabs. Its members formed a tightly knit group — known as the Lovers of Peace — all devoted to Cabbalistic studies, mystic meditation, pious living and good deeds. Their founding covenant drawn up in 1757 by one of the first Yemenites to return to the Holy Land, Rabbi Shalom Shar'abi, enjoined upon them austere rules of saintliness.

The deed, affixed to the doors of the Holy Ark, and signed by all founding members, read *inter alia*: "With the help of God and His succour, as the Lord desires penitence and contrition, the spirit moved us, the youngest of His flock, to be like one man, brethren for the sanctification of

His holy name, to gladden our Creator, upon which we have made this Covenant among us..., that we all be attached to one another, in great love of body and soul, to gladden our Creator... and if God forbid an affliction befall one of us to aid him in common... and we further undertake that every rule or restriction or good custom upon which the majority of the brethren will be of accord, shall be binding upon all and each of us to observe and live by it... and we further undertake that none of us shall pride himself on his wisdom... and if one sins to his brother the latter shall forthwith forgive him with all his heart and soul..."

At the bottom of this way of life lies the belief that the Creator and His creation, man and the grain of sand, each depend on and stand in need of the other. Prayer is the key to union in this universe and devotional practices, in many ways unique, accordingly developed in the Beit El synagogue.

There were none of the elaborate poetical embellishments grafted on the original prayer texts since medieval times. Even so services would take long hours. In Cabbalistic tradition worshippers would immerse themselves in profound meditation on every holy word and letter. They would also seek spiritual uplift, following the example of Rabbi Shar'abi, by enhancing their devotions through mystical tunes. They shunned Cabbalistic texts in print and would draw inspiration only from handwritten tracts on parchment. After days given up to study they would rise at midnight to lament the fall of the Holy Temple. At the break of dawn their beadle would, at the rabbi's bidding, climb up the roof, much like a muezzin, and call the faithful for morning devotions. They would also refrain from worldly talk and take upon themselves frequent fasts—all this to hasten the advent of Messiah.

In due course Beit El became a focus for the spiritual life of other Sephardi communities, though not for them alone. Indeed, the congregation kept its gates open to all comers and attracted seekers of mystic truth also from among the Ashkenazi. Its renowned worshippers included such widely contrasting figures as the Lithuanian rabbi Menachem Mendel of Shklow, one of the disciples of the Gaon of Vilna, a talmudist far removed from Cabbalistic practices; the Jerusalem born "Chida," Rabbi Chaim Yosef David Azulai, scion of an old Rabbinic family of Spanish origin, and famous in his own right as an outstanding scholar and bibliographer; and the German rabbi Yehoseph Schwartz from a small town in Bavaria who came to Jerusalem in 1833 to study the holy law as well as Cabbala from the scholars of Beit El and later wrote a famous work on the geography and customs of the Land of Israel.

To contribute to the maintenance of Beit El synagogue a foundation was set up in 1887 by Moshe Hacohen Hadar and his sons Abraham and Yaakov. A tablet over the entrance to the so-called Yemenite Compound on the road to the Western Wall records: "This compound has been dedicated for all time to the Beit El congregation provided that it shall not be sold or mortgaged in any way and that its yearly rental collected shall be applied to pay for rent of the above mentioned Beit El synagogue and everything shall be executed as laid down in the foundation deed according to all its conditions..."

Such provision for the support of the pious was common practice in Jerusalem, though it did not always go very far. In this case, for instance, we know that, although they would never complain, the last congregants in the 1940's suffered great want. Even so they clung to their place of worship right until that fateful day of May 28, 1948, when the last defenders of the Jewish Quarter were forced to surrender to the Jordanian Legion.

JERUSALEM'S MEMORABLE SHRINES WERE NOT ALL of impressive dimensions. Some would scarcely catch the eye of the uninitiated visitor. Yet it was often in such humble abodes that piety and inspiration found their purest expression. A moving example were the austere quarters of Or Hachaim — "The Light of Life."

This seat of esoteric studies and saintly worship derived its name from one of the venerable figures of North African Jewry, Rabbi Chaim ben Attar. An authority alike on Talmudic law and Cabbalistic lore, this eminent Bible commentator, generally referred to as Baal Or Hachaim, determined in 1733 to leave his native Morocco and settle in the Land of Israel. Passing through Leghorn, the famous traveller was prevailed upon by the wealthy congregation to interrupt his journey in order to preside over a yeshiva established especially for him and to have his *magnum opus* published at their expense. But neither honour nor rewards could keep him from making good his plans. In 1741 he proceeded to the Holy City at the head of a faithful band of followers, fortified by a promise of support from the local notables for his projected yeshiva in Jerusalem.

EIT-EL SYNAGOGUE,
view of desolation

e place
he Mezuzah

TIFERET-ISRAEL SYNAGOGUE
"An imposing landmark had been added to the Old City"

After clearing the rubble — the main entrance and facade
Left: entrance to the Karaite Compound

TIFERET-ISRAEL SYNAGOGUE
All that remained in June 1967

HABAD BROTHERHOO[D]
"Rebuilding an archwa[y]

The premises chosen were modest enough. They consisted of a handful of diminutive rooms, huddled around a scant courtyard, and with a ritual bath in the cellar beneath. The study room had a deep niche in which the rabbi would seclude himself and periodically deliver his lectures. But after his demise the niche was walled up so that no one might presume to occupy the hallowed seat. Similarly, a second Holy Ark was added to the front wall of the synagogue — a feature without precedent — to deny access to the place where the holy man used to stand in prayer.

In accordance with Sephardi custom, the core of the student body was made up originally of ten accomplished scholars to ensure an advanced level of studies. Attached to them were younger disciples. The curriculum included an exceptional feature — frequent visits to holy tombs to partake of the divine inspirations dwelling on them. On one such occasion, according to the testimony of "Chida" (Chaim Joseph David Azulai), the rabbi arrested himself at the grave of his keen scholarly rival Chiskiah de Silva to crave posthumous forgiveness for his literary attacks on him: they had been prompted by none but religious motives.

In the words of a contemporary: "his holiness was that of an angel of the Lord, having severed all connections with the affairs of this world." No wonder that the rabbi's fame spread far and wide. In the remote Carpathian Mountains the Baal Shem Tov, the founder of Chassidism, had a vision that from the Maghreb lands a saintly man had reached Jerusalem, a spark of Messiah, though unaware himself of his calling. His impact would not wane for centuries. Barely a generation ago a Yemenite patriarch was still observed prostrating himself to let his tears flow over the threshold on which the rabbi's foot had trod. And tradition has it that a follower of the Gaon of Vilna used to sweep the prayer room with his long red beard.

Numerous other such tales have come down to us; and though some may be legendary rather than historically true, all can be taken as an authentic reflection of the unique atmosphere which grew up around Or Hachaim. We are told, for instance, that the Sultan, in disguise, once betook himself to the holy man to have discourse with him on matters of faith. Or, one Sabbath eve a hundred years later the Effendi landlord burst into the prayer room, pouring abuse on the assembled congregation, forbidding the resumption of services on the morrow, and demanding that the keys be handed over to him to lock up the synagogue. Unruffled by the intruder, the rabbi replied: "This is our holy day of rest on which we will have no disputes. But let us meet before the Kadi after the Sabbath, may Allah save the Sultan." The next morning a contrite crowd of neighbours turned up to protest their innocence and beg the worshippers' pardon: the offender had passed away that very night. They beseeched the bewildered Elders to carry on their prayers as before and to implore the Lord for mercy.

Many years later a member of the same Moslem family again insisted on having the synagogue closed down. The Jews refused to submit to the challenge but declared their willingness to deliver him the keys so that he might do the deed with his own hand. Taken aback, the young man remembered what had befallen his ancestor and withdrew in consternation.

It was not given to the Baal Or Hachaim to dwell in Zion for very long. Less than ten months after his arrival he was summoned to the Yeshiva of Heaven. He was survived by two wives, both childless, who continued to live in Jerusalem until they were laid to rest at his side. The elder one, Pazzonia, is reputed to have performed her morning service like a man, wrapped in a prayer shawl and putting on phylacteries, as legend reports of Michal, daughter of Saul.

The untimely departure of the rabbi inevitably stunted the growth of his select academy. For a while funds kept flowing from its sponsors in Leghorn, yet in the end the students dispersed. But there was a revival, and in due course this small courtyard became the cradle of the city's Ashkenazi community. Its ups and downs may well give food for thought on the changing relationships between the two major branches of Jewry. It has become fashionable these days, not the least in Israel, to look down upon Sephardi Jews as "Orientals," implying their inherent inferiority. If proof were needed of the shallowness of this view, it could be readily found in these pages, if only be virtue of Or Hachaim. The truth is of course that the various Jewish communities have throughout and everywhere borne the imprint of the civilizations surrounding them.

Fittingly enough, the last occupant of Or Hachaim — Shlomo David Cahane of Warsaw — also happened to be the last Ashkenazi chief rabbi of the Old City.

MISGAV LADACH HOSPITAL AND ITS SYNAGOGUE

NO ONE WHO EVER WORSHIPPED IN MISGAV LADACH, the "Refuge for the Oppressed," now reduced to a pile of rubble, is likely to forget the experience. Through its stained glass windows a peerless view unfolded. In one vast semi-circular sweep, from the north through the east to the south, the eye would range over a bewildering multitude of sanctuaries venerated by the three great faiths — in the foreground the Temple Mount encompassed by the towers and domes of churches, mosques and synagogues; beyond the city wall the Kedron brook in the Valley of Jehoshaphat where the dead shall rise on Judgement Day; further on the Pillar of Absalom and other hallowed tombs of Jewish antiquity; behind them the slopes of the Mount of Olives, capped by Mount Scopus and the hills of Bethlehem; and in the distant background the glimmering Mountains of Moab. It must have been a callous mind that was not stirred by a sight like this.

The lowly synagogue overlooking that incomparable scene formed part of the earliest Jewish hospital in the Old City. In 1835 the Paris branch of the Rothschilds established a small clinic for Jerusalem's poor, 18 beds in all and a dispensary. When the charity was later transferred to the New City, where sizable Jewish quarters had meanwhile grown up, the premises were taken over in 1888 by Misgav Ladach, a Sephardi benevolent society. Intended at the outset for members of its own community, the society soon expanded its services to provide medical aid to all comers, irrespective of religion and race. Where necessary the sick were treated in their own homes and in case of need nurses sent to them day and night. A regulation laid down: "If the patient be destitute and without resources, the foundation shall supply him, in addition to medical care and medicines, with meals and other requirements, as conditions may warrant."

Great daring and devotion were called for in those days to embark on an enterprise like this. Depressed and backward as it was, the population could only gradually be educated to modern notions of health and hygiene; and it took patience and skill to assemble a staff that was willing to shoulder the arduous task. But the challenge had to be accepted, for in the absence of Jewish services there would be missionary institutions with all the attendant risks. Undaunted by difficulties and disappointments, the pioneers of Misgav Ladach persisted; they had the gratification of overcoming all obstacles. Their sources of support, meagre as they were, derived, significantly, from the city itself, from Bukhara and Salonika, and only to a lesser degree from Europe and America.

As the hospital always remained fairly small it is the more remarkable that the need was felt for a special synagogue. But then, no Jewish hospital is conceivable without a room of prayer. Besides, the atmosphere of the place was such as to attract friends and neighbours who would combine religious services with the great *mitzvah* of visiting the sick.

In a way, the synagogue developed into what would nowadays be termed a community centre. This was due above all to the library left to it by Rabbi Haim Hezekiah Medini "who loved Misgav Ladach." Born in Jerusalem, this endearing figure reflected the traditions of Jewish scholarship at its purest. A member of the rabbinical court of Constantinople for 13 years, and chief rabbi of the Crimea for 33, he devoted himself entirely to sacred studies, educational endeavours and pious works, setting no store by public acclaim. His modesty was such that he insisted on publishing his first responsa anonymously; and it was only with difficulty that his colleagues could prevail upon him to let his 12-volume encyclopedia of Jewish law appear under his name. He refused to accept any gifts from the rich of his congregation and was satisfied to marry his daughters to plain artisans.

After his return to Jerusalem he formed a close attachment to Misgav Ladach and willed his rich collection of rabbinical works to the hospital for sale towards its upkeep. Fortunately, a generous Jewish woman of Oran, Mrs. Valenci, acquired the valuable books and dedicated them to the synagogue where they served scholars and students for half a century. Thus came about the union, under one roof, of the three eternal tenets of Judaism "Torah, Avoda, Gemilut Hassadim" — Learning, Prayer and Good Deeds.

TIFERET ISRAEL (NISSIM BAK) SYNAGOGUE

THE CONSTRUCTION OF MONUMENTAL BUILDINGS has long been a characteristic feature of organized Jewish life, and in the Land of Israel perhaps more so than elsewhere. It has been decried as an "edifice complex," but there may well be a profound justification for this penchant. Lacking in deep roots and subject to enforced mobility, Jews appear to have had a subconscious craving for a sheet anchor in bricks and mortar. The story of Jerusalem's Tiferet Israel synagogue is a case in point.

When Nissim Bak, a lay-leader of high standing, issued his appeal in 1856 for funds to erect a dignified house of prayer for the Ashkenazi Chassidim, he gave eloquent expression to this desire for permanency. "We here the communities of Israel who dwell in this city of Jerusalem under the merciful wing of our Lord the Emperor of Austria have not been privileged to rear a place of worship, but must ever lease another house from the Ismaelites to assemble in it for prayer. From year to year we are compelled to start all over again... like fugitives and vagabonds among the four corners of the city, from East to West, from North to South.

And the wise will understand that this matter is a festering sore, verily a burning wound in our flesh — may God have mercy upon us…"

The high aspirations, though, were apt at times to produce a pathetic discrepancy between aims and means. No wonder that building works of this kind tended to drag on inordinately. In fact, the site for Nissim Bak's projected synagogue had been acquired by him as long as thirteen years earlier. He had received a sum of money for the purpose from Rabbi Israel Friedman, founder of the Ruzhin-Sadigora dynasty and spiritual leader of the Chassidic community in the Holy Land, a personality of such influence that Nikolai I judged it advisable to expel him from Russia. Tradition has it that when the Czar learned of the transaction he was greatly incensed: he himself had intended to erect a church on this very plot and felt again outwitted by the rabbi.

Meanwhile delay arose from an unexpected quarter. After transfer to Jewish ownership the site was found to contain the tomb of a Moslem Sheikh. Protracted negotiations ensued to obtain permission from the Kadi to reinter the remains of the Holy Man outside the city walls. But when everything seemed settled one of the Arabs in the know took the opportunity to try and cash in on the deal. When his attempts at extortion failed he claimed that the deceased Sheikh had appeared to him in a dream, complaining about the desecration of his grave and the intended erection of a synagogue on it. A stormy demonstration forced the Kadi to withdraw the consent earlier given to the plan. However, to keep his promise to Nissim Bak, he resorted to a counter-ruse.

In his next Friday sermon at El Aqsa Mosque the Kadi

KARAITE SYNAGOGUE
Three of the thirteen tablets (one dated 1864)

Entrance leading to the "Deutscher Platz"

revealed to his flock that the Holy Man had appeared to him also with this heart-rending tale. "Allah's beloved Abraham summoned me in Paradise, protesting: Why do the sons of your nations deny from the sons of my nation the building of a house of worship? Are we not brothers? Verily, I promised our father Abraham to intercede for him and now beg of my sons to help rather than hinder this pious work so that I may rest in peace..."

But even this was not the last obstacle to be overcome. Great difficulties were encountered in securing the necessary building permit, which had to be obtained from the Sublime Porte. Repeated applications in Jerusalem, supported by the Austrian Consul Count Pizzamano and pressed by the Ruzhiner Rebbe abroad, did not avail for years. Eventually the Austrian government saw fit to intervene in Constantinople, and it was only owing to Kaiser Franz Joseph's personal interest that the *firman* was at last issued in 1858.

"And whereas we have satisfied ourselves after due investigation that the entire compound and site belongs to the synagogue and no prejudice can at any time be caused to the other nationalities and religions in the land if the synagogue be built as mentioned above, now therefore I hereby command by Royal order and grant authority to build the synagogue... and deliver to your Excellencies the Governor and Kadi of Jerusalem my Royal firman that you may permit them to build the said synagogue 40 ells in length, 25 ells in width, 18 ells in height, and of two storeys whereof the lower one shall be reserved for the rabbis, and that you shall watch that there be no let or hindrance on any part... and no payments whatsoever be exacted from them in this matter..."

There remained the biggest difficulty of all — to raise

the necessary funds. As Nissim Bak wrote: "There is nothing we can do at present for we are left penniless and starving what with the exorbitant cost of life... nor would we willingly dispatch emissaries to solicit donations... since their outlay and commissions might consume up to half of their takings... and all the while the Consul is urging us to accomplish our work speedily... for who can tell what the future holds in store?"

The campaign actually took fourteen years, owing in part to competition of similar projects, such as the construction of the Churva synagogue. Total expenses exceeded 800,000 Piasters. The biggest single gift, let it be noted, came from a Sephardi Jew, Yechezkel Sassoon of Calcutta, who contributed 14,000 Rupees. But the most august donor turned out to be no lesser a man than His Majesty the Emperor Franz Joseph.

En route for the inauguration of the Suez Canal in 1869 the Emperor set aside a day for visiting Jewish institutions in Jerusalem. On his tour he inquired about the synagogue for the construction of which he had pleaded with the Sultan, and was duly conducted to the site. Inspecting the unfinished building, the Kaiser desired to meet the architect, and when Nissim Bak presented himself as such, the following exchange took place.

"Where has Herr Bak studied his profession?"

"At his private college, if it please your Majesty."

"And has Herr Bak not learned that a synagogue ought to have a roof?"

"It has taken it off in deference to the Imperial guest."

"If so, let us hope," rejoined the Kaiser smilingly, "that the roof will soon be replaced," backing up his hope with a gift of one thousand Francs.

When the dedication of the completed synagogue took place in 1872, with Oriental pomp and circumstance, twenty-nine years had passed since the project was launched. Yet the delay had not been in vain. An imposing landmark had been added to the Old City — with professional advice, incidentally, of a Christian Russian architect who was then engaged in building a splendid Orthodox church in New Jerusalem.

In addition to its other intriguing features Tiferet Israel — "the Glory of Israel" — had one exlusive distinction: on the flat square roof surrounding the base of its dome, services could be conducted on the high holidays, and bonfires were lit on Lag Be'Omer, within sight and in earshot of the ancient Solomonic Temple. It also had the privilege of serving as one of the last positions in the forlorn defence of the Jewish Quarter in May 1948.

BEIT MENACHEM, HABAD
BROTHERHOOD

AESTHETIC MERIT IS NOT A QUALITY ONE WOULD
naturally look for among synagogues of the Old City. Its
destitute Jewish community possessed neither the material
means nor the cultural traditions that would lead one to
expect outstanding works of art. Yet one of its modest
prayer houses was a rare architectural gem; and happily,
enough has survived to cast its spell over the visitor even
today.

Erected in 1858 as a center of study, worship and commu-
nion for Jerusalem's Habad brotherhood, Beit Menachem,
as it is called, would seem at first glance to differ little from
the austere stone buildings common in the Middle East. Its
exterior indeed suggests nothing but a two-storeyed dwelling house of slightly larger dimensions than the rest. But
what an arresting experience awaits the eye once one has
climbed up its worn steps and entered the smallish square
hall.

The immediate impression is one of gentle harmony and
soothing symmetry; the eastern wall being divided into
three deep, arched niches, of which the middle one serves

as Holy Ark and the outer ones as windows; the northern and southern walls featuring similar larger recesses with windows let in; the western wall forming an arcade masking the lower women's section; all vaulted over to a height corresponding to that of the walls (a most unusual proportion); the slender ribs rising from a light console, but instead of meeting, only leading to a circular carved slab; and the vaults again interspersed with smaller round windows. Closer inspection reveals that the symmetry is but apparent, not real; and numerous minor flaws can be detected in the design. Yet curiously, such imperfections in no way detract from the sense of immaculate purity and noble inspiration which the interior conveys. One is reminded of a flower whose irregularity of form but prevents its inherent beauty from becoming obtrusive.

This felicitous effect may or may not be the result of conscious planning: it certainly fits the spirit of the congregation. An offshoot of Hassidism, the Habad trend took over many of the original aims of that popular religious movement which arose in 18th century Russia in reaction to an excessive rationalism and formalistic aridity in contemporary Judaism. Like its parent body, Habad called for the worship of God through simple prayer, artless joy, mystic fervour and sincerity of emotion. But it went further by stressing also the need for intellectual effort and concentrated meditation to approach a true conception of deity. In contrast to ordinary Hassidism, Habad placed no exclusive reliance on the charismatic powers of the rabbi, but demanded personal exertions from the initiated to attain perfection. It reasserted the importance of study and took a rigorous view of the law.

The movement thus succeeded in creating a new synthesis of traditional Judaism. Its leaders, fired by missionary zeal, assumed increasing responsibilities in the political and social fields throughout the Jewish world, and far beyond the confines of Ashkenazi Jewry. In our day Habad Hassidism may be said to represent the most vigorous trend of Jewish orthodoxy, consistent to the end and unyielding in its opposition to any form of secularization. Israel statehood has done nothing to change this attitude, and the many flourishing Habad institutions and settlements in the country like elsewhere in the Jewish World, are based strictly on religious premises, in expectation of the advent of Messiah.

Habad attachment to the Land of Israel found early expression in 1820 when Rabbi Dov Ber of Lubawitz urged a group of his faithful to settle in Hebron, the burial place of the patriarchs. The advice was less surprising than it might appear, for Jerusalem had never been the exclusive target for pilgrimage. Indeed, after their expulsion from Spain, increasing numbers of refugees had joined the existing Jewish communities in Safad, Tiberias and Hebron, apart from Jerusalem. Each of those towns had its own traditions and shrines. Each was invested with the same degree of holiness. Each also claimed special consideration in regard to support from the Diaspora. Eventually a key for the distribution of funds was worked out in common to ensure an equitable share for each of the Four Countries of Life, as they came to be known.

Nevertheless, Jerusalem retained its unequalled hold on the hearts of Jews. In due course part of the Habad congregation of Hebron transferred to the Holy City, with the blessing of their new spiritual leader Rabbi Menachem Mendel Shneurson, and opened a humble prayer room of their own in what is still called Habad Street. As the community grew by further influx from Russia, the need was felt for more spacious premises. The required building funds were obtained from the noted philanthropist David Sassoon of Bombay, who also financed the construction of a Habad synagogue at Hebron — another example of the harmonious relationship prevailing between Sephardi and Ashkenazi Jews in those days.

The man who succeeded in securing the gift was Rabbi Shneur Zalman, son of Menachem Mendel, probably the most indefatigable and widely travelled of all Habad emissaries. Equipped with recommendations from the Baghdad branch of the prestigious Sassoon family, he visited India twice. His second journey in 1858 coincided with the Indian rebellion, which prompted him to compose a Hebrew prayer for the welfare of Queen Victoria. The gesture was graciously acknowledged in London, providing the rabbi with an entrée to Buckingham Palace and with royal letters of introduction which stood him in good stead on subsequent missions to the East. His close and cordial association with the Indian Sassoons is reflected in the choice of emblem for his stationery — an etching of the Sassoon synagogue in Bombay.

A tablet recording the generosity of David Sassoon, and enjoining that Beit Menachem must never be sold or mortgaged, has been preserved *in situ*; and history has dealt kindly with the building. In World War I, when thousands of Palestine Jews were expelled by the Turkish authorities as enemy aliens, the synagogue fell into desuetude, but served as a shelter for the Jewish poor. It was rededicated after British forces under General Allenby took the city in 1917. The ground floor was later turned over by Habad to the

Mughrabi congregation of North African Jews, and the two communities, so different in background and character, henceforth co-existed amicably under one roof.

Alone, among synagogues of the Jewish Quarter, Beit Menachem, though callously desecrated, survived nineteen years of Jordanian depredations in a state which allowed for its prompt restoration. It had the distinction of housing the first regular *minyan* to be held in Liberated Jerusalem, and the privilege of offering a place of worship to President Shazar, himself a life-long fervent follower of Habad.

GUARDIANS OF THE WALLS
(SHOMREI HACHOMOT): OHEL YITZHAK
AND BEIT JOSEPH SYNAGOGUES

ONE NIGHT IN OCTOBER 1946, RIGHT AFTER THE
Yom Kippur fast, eleven kibbutzim were set up in the
Negev wastes, in defiance of the British White Paper pro-
hibiting Jewish settlement in the area. When word reached
the authorities in the morning, there was nothing they
dared do about it. The operation actually followed a pattern
evolved in the 'thirties. To guard against interference by
Arab rioters the settlers in those years would move, under
cover of darkness, to the site, bringing up prefabricated
parts of a watch tower, stockade, tents and huts to be
assembled by daybreak

Even that system had its precedent. One generation
before, at the turn of the century, two synagogues were a-
building in the Old City with the permission of the muni-
cipality. Work had proceeded to a stage where only the
roof remained to be constructed. All of a sudden a restrain-
ing order arrived from the Kadi, claiming that the Moslem
population were opposed to the erection of a synagogue
at the approaches to the Dome of the Rock. The builders,
a congregation of Hungarian Jews known as Guardians of

the Walls, took counsel and determined to avail themselves of a loophole: under the Ottoman code no roofed-in building, whether erected legally or other-wise, must be demolished. Accordingly, one dark night the entire congregation — men, women and children — turned up with the necessary tools and materials and in a burst of feverish activity and high enthusiasm finished the job before sunrise.

The Arab neighbours never forgave them their daring. Although no legal steps could be taken to remove the offense the buildings became the target for frequent molestations and infringements, culminating in their destruction during the 1929 disturbances. What remained of the pillage was later transferred to the Mea Shearim quarter in the New City.

While belonging to the same congregation and being in a way twins, the two synagogues, located in one courtyard, provided for two different trends. One, Ohel Yitzhak, served the Hassidim; the other, Beit Joseph, their opponents the Mitnagdim, or as they used to be called in Jerusalem, Perushim. The two denominations differed not only in temperament and philosophy, but in ritual and style of worship. Each attached such significance to every single word and turn of phrase in its liturgy that, notwithstanding their identical background and basic agreement on beliefs, common services were impossible.

The largest, most enterprising and most successful of all Ashkenazi groups in Jerusalem, the Guardians of the Walls, were of relatively recent origin. Their beginnings date back to the forties of the 19th century. Their moving spirit was Chatam Sofer, who, born in Frankfurt on the Main, yet became undisputed leader of the extremist Hungarian orthodoxy and, as head of the Pressburg yeshiva, a universally recognized authority on talmudic law. They were preceded by earlier settlers from Safad who fled the city struck by a violent earthquake in 1837 — a catastrophe which the rabbi regarded as a heavenly punishment for their failure to make their home in the Holy City. Among those who came from Europe some had made the whole way on foot: the arduous journey was considered a meritorious deed, which incidentally gave Jewish communities through which the pilgrims passed an opportunity to share in their inspired undertaking.

As their numbers grew through sustained immigration, the group eventually set up its own Kolel (welfare federation) in 1858, breaking away from the general body of Ashkenazi Jewry in Jerusalem. Their secession climaxed a development which had been gathering momentum for several decades. Since ancient times the impoverished remnant in the Land of Israel, and those returning to it, had been aided by their brethren in the Diaspora. For centuries the contributions collected by emissaries all over the Jewish world had been distributed to the needy irrespective of their communal affiliations — a principle reconfirmed by the rabbis of Venice in 1601. Yet gradually pressures built up on the part of interested landsmanshaften for an increased share of the takings. A division became unavoidable, in the first instance, between Sephardis and Ashkenazis, and further subdivisions by countries of birth or former residence within the Ashkenazi community from the late 18th century onwards. Among the more important Kolel organizations were those of the Dutch and German ("Hod") and of the Warsaw Jews. The formation of the Hungarian Kolel set the seal to this process of fragmentation, with its inevitable inequities to the poor groups, but also with its undeniable advantages to fund raising as a whole.

It might be pointed out, in passing, that the Hebrew term for this sytem of support, "Halukka," corresponds almost literally to the name of its latter-day big brother the JDC (Joint Distribution Committee).

For all their attachment to the Old City, only a minority of the Guardians lived within its walls to keep services going in their two prayer houses day and night — a practice called "watches" (*mishmorim* in Hebrew). The bulk could find no dwellings in the all but Moslem neighbourhood and were forced to build for themselves an extensive quarter outside the walls. But they would make it a point of honour to worship on Sabbath days and festivals in their own cherished synagogues, closer than any other to the Temple Mount. The fervour of their devotions and the compelling atmosphere of the place attracted even outsiders. S. Y. Agnon would join the congregants for the Day of Atonement, from Kol Nidrei to the closing shofar blast. His admiration for their prayer leader moved him to set this monument in his writings:

"Rabbi Katriel the Reader was among the last of the pious in Jerusalem who, sparing of their own concerns and lavish in the praise of heaven, were established in the seat of learning to delve into the Scriptures and the oral law, into rabbinical rulings and sacred tales, ponder the secrets of the Torah and the traditions of the sages, proclaim the justice and mercy of the Holy One, blessed be He, every day and at all times, sanctify His great name in the world with all their deeds, thoughts and strength, bewail the profanation of His glory among the heathen and the denial of honour to Israel, with their minds and hearts set upon the splendour of Jerusalem, the Temple and the Land of Israel when the exiles will gather in and the Holy One, blessed be He, bring back His dwelling to Zion. For as long as Israel be scattered among the nations, oppressed and despised by them, God grieves for His people and the pious take His grief to heart and writhe before Him, blessed be He, so that He may turn His mercy on His chosen sons, the flocks of His pasture, the seed of Abraham His lover, the sons of Isaac His only one, the family of Jacob His first born, since there will be no restoring the Holy Presence save through the redemption of Israel." *

* Translated from "Rabbi Katriel", Schocken, Jerusalem, 1942, vol. 8, pp. 36–37 (by permission of the publisher).

THE PORAT JOSEPH YESHIVA

IN THE LONG CHAIN OF ENDEAVOURS TO REVIVE Jewish settlement in the Old City, the last significant link was the Porat Joseph yeshiva. Conceived in 1911 and completed in 1923, after unavoidable delays during World War I, its construction coincided with the growth of Jewish Jerusalem outside the walls. Nothing might have seemed more natural therefore than to put up this magnificent modern building in more convenient surroundings. But mere convenience carried no weight with its founder Joseph Abraham Shalom, of Calcutta, as indeed it was not the motive force of his countless predecessors. What impelled Jews throughout the ages to acquire a stake in the Old City was something rather less mundane — proximity to their holy places.

"How much did I labour and toil with body and soul (says the dedication tablet in the synagogue) until the Lord privileged me to build this glorious shrine on the heights of Mount Zion facing the Holy Temple and its Western Wall... to establish the law in Zion and God's word in

Jerusalem at this holy place of which it is said: My eyes and My heart shall be there all the days."

Paradoxically, this last and most impressive monument to Sephardi Jewry to be reared in the Old City also coincided with the community's temporary decline. Its declared purpose was indeed to restore the proud traditions of that community not only in the Land of Israel but throughout the Jewish world. From the early Middle Ages well down into Modern Times this branch of the Jewish people had never been challenged in its pre-eminence intellectually, socially or politically. But with the progressive eclipse of the Mediterranean and especially Moslem countries and the concomitant rise of Central Europe and America, accompanied by the gradual emergence of Ashkenazi Jewry, it lost much of its vigour and prominence. The Sephardi leadership could conceive of no surer way to bring about renewed interest and action than the founding of a talmudic academy. In this they reflected the course of Jewish history which had always demonstrated learning as the mainspring of renascence. There is perhaps no analogy in other civilizations to this intimate relationship between religious fervour and intellectual exercise: one depending for its fulfilment on the other. The classical type of synagogue was never a Jewish kind of church, devoted exclusively to spiritual uplift. It had a second function of equal importance: to serve as a place of study and debate. In fact, instruction in the law formed an integral part of services, as a link between different prayers or as an epilogue to them. This singular combination, incidentally, brought with it a sort of casualness and lack of decorum which at times upset observers not familiar with the ways of Jewish worship.

The very lay-out of Porat Joseph provided a perfect

illustration of those twin aspects of Judaism. Its centre piece, the stately synagogue graced with a dome borne by marble pillars, was enclosed with study rooms of every description — on the top floor the main auditorium of the yeshiva and eight classrooms, in the two broad wings flanking the synagogue a library, a smaller prayer room for the training of cantors, further lecture halls and study rooms, offices and dormitories, and on another two floors below more dormitories as well as spacious apartments for the teaching staff. It is worth noting that the relatively modernistic, if timeless, style of the building blended in remarkable harmony with the variegated background of Oriental and European edifices.

Another rare feature deserves mention. It is customary nowadays for benefactors to raise magnificent structures bearing their names, but not to make provision for upkeep and running costs. The founder of Porat Joseph thought otherwise. He set up a trust fund with which to maintain the entire student body and academic staff and meet all other expenses. No one admitted to this yeshiva was prevented by material cares from applying his undivided attention to the pursuit of learning. The endowment left was sufficient to cover the full needs until 1941, when inflation on an unforeseen and unforeseeable scale took its toll and supplementary sources of support had to be tapped.

The noble undertaking did not, alas, endure. Situated on the very borderline of the Jewish Quarter, it always suffered from infringements by its Arab neighbours. Towards the end of the Mandate it was occupied by British forces. In 1948, on the heels of the departing troops, the Jews again took possession of this strategic post. They became the immediate target for an overwhelming bombardment but held on to the crumbling building until their retreat to the adjoining Batei Machse compound. Even after the fall of the Jewish Quarter the Jordanian Legion and civilian population continued to wreck the scant remains of Porat Joseph, turning it into an utter ruin.

THE KARAITE SYNAGOGUE

THIRTY-SIX FROM AMONG THE SYNAGOGUES OF THE
Old City are described, in varying detail, in a symposium
published by the Ministry of Religious Affairs of the State
of Israel in 1955. But not so much as mention is made of
the existence of the most ancient of all — that of the Karaites. This curious omission can scarcely be accidental. It
doubtlessly reflects the attitude of official Judaism to this
all but extinguished sect.

Nor is this surprising. There were times when the Rabbanite trend of Judaism — the only one regarded nowadays
as legitimate — found itself fiercely challenged by the rival
Karaite trend and had to fight back for its very survival.
The issue, put in modern terms, was that of orthodoxy
versus reform; and the outcome a victory for reform which
in due course turned into a new kind of orthodoxy.

Stripped from its later and self-contradictory develop-
ments, the essence of Karaism was a return to scriptural
purity. Its scholars based themselves on the Biblical dictum
"Ye shall not add unto the word which I command you,
neither shall ye diminish ought from it" (Deut. IV, 2). They

categorically rejected the Oral Law which, according to Rabbanite tradition, had been handed down together with the Written Law, elaborating, interpreting and developing the latter in a continuous effort to adapt it to the changing conditions of life. Their opposition to the Talmudic leadership also had social undertones. It expressed the resentment of aggrieved and destitute Palestinian Jewry under Omayyad rule to their prosperous and powerful brethren in Mesopotamia who, in the rigorist view of Karaism, sought to ease the "burdens" of religion by adroit legalistic justification for their laxity.

The redoubtable founder of the sect, Anan Ben David of Baghdad, led his zealots to Jerusalem in the eighties of the 8th century, making the city the centre of militant Karaism. From there the movement spread to Egypt, Syria, Persia, the Crimea, and later to Spain, Lithuania and Galicia. Wherever it sprang up, passionate and acrimonious polemics followed in its wake, causing the eventual decline of Karaite communities whether through return to Rabbanite Judaism or through conversion to Islam or Christianity.

The origins of the Karaite synagogue in Jerusalem go far back into antiquity. A tablet affixed in the year 1864 claims that it was established by Anan himself, but the few literary references extant do not permit us to date the building before the end of the 11th century, when the sect had reached the acme of its influence. This conclusion is strengthened by the evidence of the cross vaults of its ceiling and other architectural details. It is clear at any rate that this was the oldest house of prayer surviving in the Jewish Quarter before its destruction in 1948.

Actually, it was more than a synagogue. Around it other houses were built, all primitive and small, which served as dwellings for the community; their ruins can still be discerned. The whole compound was enclosed by a wall, as usual in Oriental cities, to provide protection against depredations of robbers — a fact, incidentally, which fitted the sect's sense of living as a minority.

Strictly speaking, it might be more correct to describe the Karaite synagogue as an elaborate cave. To reach its floor one had to climb down as much as 4.70 meters of steep steps from the courtyard. There were no windows in it: according to tradition, they had been expressly forbidden by the Moslem authorities. For many long centuries no sun-ray could penetrate, and it was only two hundred years ago that three chimney-shaped shafts were broken into the roof, letting in a modicum of light and air. Even then the almost exclusive source of lighting remained candles.

Notwithstanding its diminutive size the synagogue had an anteroom where all worshippers would take off their shoes. This custom seems to indicate Islamic influence, which is recognizable also in other aspects of Karaite lore. The prayer room proper had a wooden floor, in contrast to the normal stone or marble floors of other Jerusalem synagogues. It was covered with plain straw mats on weekdays, and with colourful carpets on the Sabbath and festivals. Attached to the synagogue was a *mikve* bath, used for ritual immersion before certain prayers. It drew its water from an adjacent deep cistern which served the residents of the courtyard until recent times.

One more architectural peculiarity deserves to be recorded. By Jewish custom synagogues throughout the world are built in such a way that the Holy Ark faces towards the Land of Israel, in Israel to Jerusalem, and in Jerusalem itself to the presumed centre of the Temple

Mount. In contradistinction to this the Karaite synagogue is directed roughly to the Wailing Wall, the last remains of the outer enclosure of the Temple Compound.

In its last stage the dwindling community could no longer muster the required prayer quorum of ten. Nevertheless, they would assemble for services once a week, on the Sabbath. In fact, there were not even seven men to be called to the seven portions of the weekly reading of the Law. The pathetic expedient was therefore adopted of two or three men taking turns in going up to the Torah. To pronounce the blessing they used to prostrate themselves full length on the floor.

Since 1755 the Karaites of Jerusalem have believed that they are doomed by a curse. In that year the Turkish authorities imposed a heavy head-tax on all Jews in the city. To take counsel on the oppressive edict the Elders convened a secret meeting in the underground synagogue of the Karaites. Descending the narrow steps, the chief rabbi slipped and fell down fainting. The incident gave rise to a terrified search for evil ghosts, in the course of which the codex of Maimonides was discovered hidden under the staircase: it had been placed there by the Karaites with the intent of having everyone tread on it by way of contempt. Outraged by the blasphemy, the rabbi cursed the offending community to be reduced to less than a *minyan*.

When a group of Karaites came from the Crimea in later years, all, according to tradition, were stricken by disease and died to the last man. Since then even occasional pilgrims would refrain from staying overnight in the accursed courtyard. Yet pilgrimages did not cease. As many as thirteen tablets were preserved, and some are still on site, commemorating visits from Egypt, Constantinople, St.

Petersburg and other places. The last Karaites to reach Israel came from Egypt in the wake of the Sinai Campaign of 1956, almost twelve centuries after the rise of the sect.

In Memoriam

Shimon Ben-Eliezer

DR. SHIMON BEN-ELIEZER, who died in Jerusalem a month ago at the age of 62, was an outstanding civil servant of the Jewish people. As assistant to three successive treasurers of the Jewish Agency he commanded an encyclopedic knowledge of that body's far-flung operations.

The personality and career of Ben-Eliezer — born Siegfried Koesterich — in many ways symbolized the unique contribution of the German immigrant to the life of the country. Functioning in a milieu where public relations was all-important, Ben-Eliezer's modesty and self-effacement were such that few beyond his im-

· 63 ·

mediate circle even knew his name. A man of uncompromising integrity, temperamentally quite unsuited for politics, he yet had a sophisticated understanding of the game as it is played in Israel, and he served the political figures who were his superiors with unswerving loyalty and frequently affection. Educated in Britain, equally at home in both German and English, he became in mature adulthood an accomplished stylist in Hebrew. He was a cosmopolitan who fervently believed in the Jewish homeland, an Israeli patriot with an instinctive distaste of chauvinism, and a tradionalist whose religion was free of dogmatism. His ideologically consistent Zionism necessarily included *Shlilat ha-Golah* (rejection of the Diaspora), yet he became an unusually effective communicator between Israel and the Jews of America.

Perhaps the climax of his career was his role as a principal architect of the Conference on Human Needs which took place in Jerusalem in 1969, and which in an important sense paved the way for the reconstitution of the Jewish Agency.

In the mid-'fifties, Ben-Eliezer took a leave from the Agency to implement a long-cherished idea of his: the publication of an Israeli English-language weekly. With its mixture of serious reportage, urbane commentary and political satire, the journal he edited was a *succes d'estime* but a financial failure; looking back, it is apparent that "Here and Now" was ahead of its time. Some years later, the Overseas Weekly of *The Jerusalem Post* came along to fill the then obvious need.

Among Ben-Eliezer's personal attributes were a rare capacity for friendship and an impish sense of humour, both of which remained undefeated in the most difficult times of failing health.

Dr. Ernest Stock

(From Jerusalem Post, July 21, 1971)